UFOs

BY

JOHN DUNCAN

ANCIENT UFOS

"**I**n the 30th year, in the 4th month, on the 5th day, by the river Chebar," wrote the prophet Ezekiel in the Bible, "I saw something that looked like burning coals of fire." Ezekiel described how he saw wheels sparkle like jewels, "being as it were a wheel within a wheel." Ezekiel saw his experience as a vision of God. UFOlogists would say it was one of the first recorded sightings of an unidentified flying object (UFO).

ALIEN FOOTPRINT

This fossilized *hominid* (human-like) footprint from East Africa was made by a creature that walks on two legs. Yet the rock is 3.5 million years old! Some UFOlogists claim the footprint was made before *Homo erectus* (prehistoric man) appeared. They claim that it was made by a visiting spaceman.

ANCIENT ABDUCTIONS

Celtic (ancient Irish) legends told of fairies who stole babies from their cribs. The fairies replaced the human babies with fairy infants. To keep their babies safe, medieval peasants hung a knife over the cradle. Were these "fairies" alien scientists?

PREHISTORIC RECORDS

These prehistoric rock drawings from Peru seem to show astronauts wearing space helmets. Cave paintings sometimes show discs in the sky. The Bible tells us that in prehistory "the sons of God" came down and married human women. Could these be ancient stories about visits by spacemen?

A DESERT MYSTERY

Over 1,000 years ago, in Nazca, Peru, thousands of stones were arranged to make long lines and huge figures in the desert. The images, including these "aliens," are easy to see from the air. However, they are difficult to see while standing beside them. In 1969, the writer Erich von Däniken suggested that "ancient astronauts" visited Earth. They changed humankind's technology and genes and shaped human history. He claimed that these Nazca lines were made to be seen by alien visitors from their spaceships.

CULTURAL TRACKING

A Bible story tells of the prophet Elijah being carried away by a chariot of fire. In 1897, people saw airships in the sky. In the 1950s metal spaceships were seen (see pages 4–5). UFOs seem to appear in whatever form people expect to see them. This may account for the wide variety of reported sightings.

FAMOUS SIGHTINGS IN HISTORY

c. 1450 BCE, EGYPT

Pharaoh Thutmose III sees "circles of fire" in the sky.

322 BCE, LEBANON

Shining silver shields fly over a city being attacked by Alexander the Great. They destroy the walls by firing beams of light at the defenses.

840 CE, FRANCE

The Archbishop of Lyons stops people killing two creatures who had come to Earth in a "cloud ship."

1211, IRELAND

The people of Cloera try to catch creatures whose "airship" had caught on their church roof.

1271, JAPAN

The execution of a Buddhist monk is called off when a bright object hangs in the sky above the site.

1492, ATLANTIC OCEAN

A sailor on Columbus's ship, the Santa Maria, sees a glittering thing in the sky.

1639, BOSTON, MASSACHUSETTS

Mr. James Everell and friends are fishing when a bright light floats over them and moves their boat upstream.

1752, SWEDEN

Farmers see a large, shining object in the sky "give birth" to smaller balls of light.

1762, SWITZERLAND

In different towns, two astronomers independently record a "spindle-shaped" aircraft move across the face of the sun.

1819, MASSACHUSETTS

Professor Rufus Graves sees a fireball crash into the yard of his friend Erastus Dewey. They find wreckage and, inside it, a stinky pulpy substance.

1820, USA

Mormon leader Joseph Smith sees a UFO and talks with beings inside it.

1861, CHILE

Peasants see a metal bird with shining eyes and scales.

1868, ENGLAND

Astronomers at the Radcliffe Observatory, Oxford University, track a UFO for 4 minutes.

1887, BANJOS, SPAIN

Villagers find two "children" in a cave. Their clothes are strange, they speak no known language, and their skin is green.

SIGHTINGS

UFOs definitely exist. What is in doubt is what they are. Every year, over a thousand sightings are reported. Many sightings are reported by people who ask to remain *anonymous* (unnamed). They don't want other people to think they are crazy. Famous people who have seen UFOs include two presidents. President Jimmy Carter once watched a UFO while he was at a dinner party. President Ronald Reagan surprised a White House meeting by announcing he had once seen a UFO from the window of his plane. Astronaut Major Gordon Cooper reported seeing a glowing green object on his space flight in 1963. That object had also appeared on Australian radar. In 1965, spacewalkers Ed White and James McDivitt reported seeing a metallic UFO. It had "arms" sticking out in all directions.

 ## FOOD FOR THOUGHT

In the 1960s, the United States Air Force Project Blue Book studied 13,000 UFO sightings. It found that only about 2 percent were really unidentified. Most UFOs are natural phenomena (events). Explanations include:

- *Aircraft and satellites.*
- *Weather balloons.*
- *Jupiter and other planets that are often unusually bright. A trick of the eye called autokinesis can make them seem to move in the sky.*
- *Meteors.*
- *Earthquakes. Canadian scientists have found a connection between UFO sightings and earthquakes. Stress on rocks just before an earthquake can produce strong electrical fields and strange lights.*
- *Vitreous floaters (matter moving inside the eye itself).*
- *Wishful thinking, hysteria, and emotional disturbance.*

Yes, it is less romantic! But even the UFO sightings not yet explained are likely to fall into a category of natural phenomena. There are still a lot of natural events that we don't yet fully understand (such as ball lightning). Or they may be related to military experiments.

ALIEN WARFARE

This woodcut (picture cut into wood) from 1561 records a frightening event in Germany. That year, black and red balls of light seemed to battle together in the sky. Some UFOlogists suggest that maybe two kinds of aliens were fighting for control of Earth.

A UFO OF THE NINETIES

Jeremy Johnson, who took this photograph in England in 1992, thought at first he had missed his chance. The round white object vanished as soon as he pointed the camera at it.

THE AIRSHIP PHENOMENON

In 1897, many people saw shining, cigar-shaped "airships." This picture was drawn for a newspaper at the time. A man named E.J. Pennington said the airship belonged to him. But nobody would believe that they were seeing an actual airship and not a UFO!

The Flying Saucer as I Saw it... by Kenneth Arnold

TUNGUSKA DISASTER

In 1908, an explosion in Siberia, Russia, flattened trees for miles around. No meteor or crater was found. Modern theories of the cause include a comet or a small black hole. Local people, however, described an oval fireball that rose up from the ground. They experienced an illness like radiation sickness. UFOlogists suggest the phenomenon was an exploding spaceship.

UFOLOGY IS BORN

One sighting that got a lot of attention was made by Kenneth Arnold. In June 1947, Arnold saw nine V-shaped UFOs near Mt. Rainier in Washington. He told a newspaper reporter that they moved at speeds of over 1,000 mph (1,600 km/h). He said they moved "like a saucer would if you skipped it across the water." The newspaper's report of "Flying Saucers" captured the public's imagination. *Fate Magazine* was published a year later. It was the first of many UFO books and magazines.

FOO FIGHTERS

During World War II, many British and American pilots reported seeing small shining discs (which they called "foo fighters"). These discs followed planes and made the engines short out. One UFOlogist thought these discs were remotely-controlled alien probes. This World War II photograph clearly shows these mysterious discs in the sky.

THE ROSWELL INCIDENT

This artist's drawing of the Roswell incident shows a UFO being struck by lightning in a storm on July 4, 1947.

 FOOD FOR THOUGHT

There may be a simpler reason for the U.S. government's refusal to admit that an alien spaceship crashed in Roswell. They may have been trying to keep secret a Japanese "balloon bomb" left over from World War II. Another top-secret device was a U.S. "spy-balloon" designed to keep an eye on Russia's nuclear weapons program. In 1947, the U.S. Air Force bomber group at Roswell was the world's only nuclear-armed strike force. It is almost certain that the government secrecy was to keep enemy countries from learning about these military operations.

THE TRUTH IS OUT THERE

On July 8, 1947, local engineer Grady Barnett added to the Roswell mystery. He and a team of archaeologists claimed to have found a crashed disc-shaped UFO. They also said they found the bodies of four aliens. They described the aliens as small, gray, and human-shaped with large heads. The U.S. Air Force quickly removed these, leaving nothing to be seen. Even an investigation by the U.S. Senate in 1994 failed to convince some people that the government was not holding back evidence. Those people want to believe that the government is hiding the wreckage of a UFO and the bodies of aliens.

The idea of a secret UFO is so attractive that it is impossible to get rid of such beliefs. People are excited about what we might learn by copying the design of a crashed spaceship

THE MOST FAMOUS UFO

On July 4, 1947, there was a lightning storm over the town of Roswell in New Mexico. Sitting in his farmhouse, rancher William "Mac" Brazel thought he heard an explosion. The next day, Brazel rode out to check his sheep. He discovered some wreckage "like nothing made on Earth." It crumpled like foil but slowly straightened itself out again. It was not damaged by blows from a sledgehammer. Brazel reported it to the local air base. He was arrested and held in custody until the wreckage had been recovered. This was the start of one of the best-known and longest-lasting UFO stories.

CAPTURED!

Since the Arnold "flying saucer" story of June 1947, the U.S. Air Force had recorded almost a thousand UFO sightings. They came from all over. There were many reports of downed spacecraft. For example, on July 8, 1947, the commander at the Roswell Air Force base told the press that a flying disc had been recovered from a site nearby. Immediately, according to the *Roswell Daily Record*, the Roswell wreckage became a crashed UFO in which four aliens had been found.

ALIEN AUTOPSY

In 1996, businessman Ray Santilli released a film on real 1947 film stock. It showed autopsies (medical examinations done after death) being done on the aliens recovered from the Roswell crash. The film was like a B-class horror movie. The aliens looked nothing like those supposedly found in the Roswell crash. There was even a modern phone clearly visible in the background. Yet UFO fans were convinced by the "evidence" of this film. This picture, from the Roswell International UFO Museum, shows a model of the alien body from the filmed "autopsy."

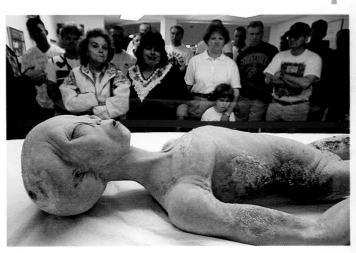

BALLOON WRECKAGE

On the afternoon of July 8, 1947, the U.S. Air Force held two press conferences. A polite, fresh-faced, and very believable young warrant officer showed foil pieces from a weather balloon. He said the balloon was the cause of the confusion. When asked if it was the remains of a flying saucer, the young man giggled. People thought the explanation was false. The government obviously wanted to cover something up. That same month, there were a number of cargo flights from Roswell to the top-secret Wright-Patterson Air Force base in Ohio. What they were carrying has never been explained well enough for skeptics to accept.

CLOSE ENCOUNTER CATEGORIES

CE1: *Sighting only*
CE2: *Some physical evidence has been left (e.g., crop circles)*
CE3: *Aliens have been seen*
CE4: *Alien abduction (kidnapping)*
CE5: *Humans and aliens have met and interacted*

 ## FOOD FOR THOUGHT

After four years, the Hessdalen investigators decided that the lights were probably a natural phenomenon. There is so much about our world that we do not understand. It is highly likely that UFOs are, in fact, a natural but rare phenomena that we cannot explain yet. Only when we understand everything about our own world will we be able to say that such events may have been caused by aliens.

CLOSE ENCOUNTERS

During the 1950s and 1960s, there were thousands of UFO sightings. It was not until 1972 that a way of *analyzing* (studying) and *categorizing* (organizing) them was developed by J. Allen Hynek. Hynek was a respected UFOlogist. In his book *The UFO Experience*, Dr. Hynek was the first UFOlogist to divide the different kinds of UFO events into types of close encounters. Ever since then, UFOlogists have classified UFO events using his categories. These range from close encounters of the first kind, to close encounters of the fifth kind. There's also a strangeness rating that measures how normal sightings are.

HESSDALEN LIGHTS

As well as photographing the lights, the researchers also used other tools to analyze the phenomenon. These included radar, seismographs (that measure earth movements), infrared viewers, spectrum analyzers, and Geiger counters (that measure radiation). Scientists wanted to see if the lights were leaving any physical evidence of their presence.

▲ A CE2: PROJECT HESSDALEN, NORWAY

During 1981–85, Norwegian scientists studied lights that appeared over Hessdalen. The lights moved and seemed to respond to the actions of the observers.

CLOSE ENCOUNTERS OF THE THIRD KIND

Steven Spielberg's 1977 film was based on UFOlogist J. Allen Hynek's book *The UFO Experience* (1972). In the story, a series of UFO encounters gradually build up to a friendly meeting between aliens and humans (a CE5). It has been suggested that the government asked Steven Spielberg to make the film to soothe public fears about UFOs.

A CE1: THE LUBBOCK LIGHTS

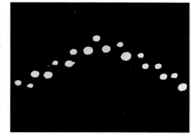

In 1951, the people of Lubbock, Texas, reported a V-shaped formation of lights passing overhead at night. The lights were said to be traveling at about 400 mph (650 km/h). A nearby radar station also recorded an "unknown" object. Official explanations of the phenomenon include a flight of geese lit by street lights, and an new jet bomber being tested in the area.

CATTLE MUTILATIONS, CROP CIRCLES & OTHER CE2s

A close encounter of the second kind happens when a UFO leaves some physical evidence of its presence. One famous example involved a French farmer from Trans-en-Provence. In 1981 he reported that an object had landed in his garden. Government investigators found the soil had been heated to 1,112°F (600°C). One scientist suggested the effects had been produced by a strong electromagnetic field. The story is like that of another farmer, M. Masse. In 1965, Masse claimed that a spaceship had landed in his lavender field in Valensole, about 30 miles (48 km) from Trans-en-Provence.

CROP CIRCLES

In the 1980s, crop circles began to appear all over the world. Most were in Britain and, as this example shows, in Japan. UFOlogists suggested they were made by landing spacecraft. The circles became very famous.

A CE2 OF A DIFFERENT KIND

Stephen Michalak, an amateur geologist, claims to have seen a spaceship near Winnipeg, Canada, in 1967. Apparently, when the craft flew away the heat was so intense that his clothes were set on fire. Later, the pattern of a grill appeared burned onto Michalak's chest. Some skeptics claimed that Michalak had burned himself. However, scientists found evidence of radioactivity and extreme heat at the landing site.

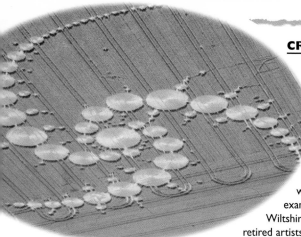

CROP ART

One Australian suggested crop circles were caused by courting coots (a type of water bird). A British expert blamed stampeding hedgehogs. A meteorologist said they were caused by stationary tornadoes. Soon, elaborate crop patterns started to appear that could not possibly have been made by the weather. This beautiful example appeared in Wiltshire, England. In 1991, two retired artists showed how they had faked many crop patterns in Britain. Strangely, many tricksters have reported seeing UFOs while they were working on the crop patterns.

HOW DID SNIPPY DIE?

In 1967, a horse called Snippy (or Lady in some accounts) was found dead on a ranch in Colorado. Her head had been skinned with a straight cut and her organs had been removed. There was no blood on the ground, and there were circle-shaped exhaust marks all around the body. Similar cases have been reported from all over the world. There were a large number of horse mutilations (damage by cutting) in England in the 1980s.

FOOD FOR THOUGHT

Why would aliens fly 2,000 light years to mess around in fields? Why would such technologically advanced beings need thousands of animal organs for their studies? These stories are so unbelievable that no one should ever think they are the work of alien visitors. The real danger is that scientists may miss the one witness who has had a real CE2. They will have been busy investigating reports by thousands of tricksters and cranks!

CATTLE MUTILATION

There have been hundreds of reports of mutilations of cattle, such as this example from New Mexico. Some people suggest they are the work of Satanists (people who worship the Devil). Examinations of individual animals have shown that the blood in the flesh on either side of the cuts has been cooked at a temperature of about 302°F (150°C). Yet the cells around the cuts remained undamaged. Today, we know of no instruments that can do this.

Aboard a Flying Saucer

by TRUMAN BETHURUM

Non-Fiction—A True Account of Factual Experience

TRUMAN BETHURUM CONTACTEE, 1954

Bethurum was a road-builder who claimed to have met aliens in the California desert near Las Vegas in 1954. His visitors had olive-green skin and dark hair. They came from Clarion, a planet that could not be seen from the Earth because it was behind the moon. Clarion, Bethurum was told, had no disease, crime, or politicians.

ABOARD A FLYING SAUCER

Bethurum claimed he had actually been taken aboard the alien spaceship. When he was there, he met the craft's captain, a beautiful alien called Aura Rhanes. She spoke in rhyme. Bethurum had romantic feelings for her. This really annoyed his wife! Bethurum wrote a successful book about his experiences.

 FOOD FOR THOUGHT

All this evidence, like all UFO evidence, is made up of the stories of individuals. It confirms UFOlogy as no more than a pseudo-science. It is based on stories and hearsay (rumors not supported by evidence). The stories are obviously ridiculous. Today, we are still interested in these stories. But we are interested in them because many people in the 1950s were easily fooled. What has changed in our society to make us less likely to believe such stories?

AN ALIEN IN NEW JERSEY, 1957

Born in 1922, Howard Menger says he first saw "space-people" as a child. He said he also had many close encounters while in the army. In his book *From Outer Space to You* (1959), he wrote about meeting Venusians. Some of them were over 500 years old. They included a number of beautiful women in see-through ski-suits. The "spacewoman" in this picture seems to be wearing a more usual spacesuit. Menger claims to have helped the Venusians fit into Earthly society. He cut the men's long hair and offered the women bras! Menger said his second wife, Marla, was from Venus. In the 1960s, Menger claimed the Central Intelligence Agency (CIA) had asked him to make up the encounters so that they could test public reaction to UFO stories. He also claimed men in black (see page 20) tried to stop him from talking about his sightings.

TAKE ME TO YOUR LEADER!

I n a close encounter of the fifth kind there is interaction (contact or talking) between aliens and humans. The 1950s saw many close encounters. During this period, many books were published on the subject. Meetings with space beings were described by a number of speakers at public lectures. Nowadays, UFOlogists are embarrassed by these stories. The stories hurt the reputation of real UFO research.

JOE SIMONTON

Many other people claimed to have met space visitors. One strange case was that of 60-year-old chicken farmer Joe Simonton of Wisconsin. In 1961, he was visited by small, dark-skinned spacemen wearing black suits and knitted caps! The aliens asked him for a jug of water, and in return gave him some pancakes. Simonton ate one of the pancakes, which tasted like cardboard. He sent the others for analysis. They were made out of ordinary flour but with no salt. Local people said Simonton was a quiet, ordinary man who did not make up strange stories.

FLYING SAUCERS HAVE LANDED

George Adamski was a waiter who later called himself a "professor." He wrote an unpublished fiction book about meeting a man from Venus. When he told people his story was true, his book, *Flying Saucers Have Landed* (1953), became a published bestseller.

GEORGE ADAMSKI
CONTACTEE, 1953

In 1953, after seeing a UFO in the California desert, Adamski went to investigate. He met a handsome, sun-tanned young Venusian with long, sandy-colored hair. The alien communicated with Adamski using hand signs and telepathy. The alien told him that Venus was Earth's sister planet. The Venusians had come to warn humanity that nuclear radiation could ruin Earth. Adamski later claimed to have been taken by his Venusian friends to Mars, Saturn, and Jupiter.

FOOD FOR THOUGHT

One in six people need psychiatric (mental health) help at some time in their adult lives. "Abduction" experiences are probably a form of mental delusion (false belief). The Hills and the Walton cases (see pages 16–17) both show how the power of television affects our subconscious minds (the thoughts we have that we are unaware of). Even under hypnosis it is possible to tell lies. There is also a lot of evidence that hypnotists can create false memories. Indeed, experiments have been done in which people were able to invent realistic "imaginary abductions" under hypnosis. People have also been observed having an abduction experience. In one case in Australia, two people watched as someone (who never left their sight) apparently met aliens and went into a spaceship. It was clearly a real event inside the head of the "abductee." However, all the two witnesses saw was that person's physical responses to what he seemed to be experiencing. Most abduction "memories" are alike. They involve tunnels, lights, being covered in liquid, finding it hard to breathe, pain in the belly button, being medically examined, etc. Women abductees remember having eggs taken from their ovaries. Occasionally they think unborn alien babies have been placed inside them. In these details, most "abductions" seem more like a flashback to the experience of being born rather than of an alien encounter.

ABDUCTION CASEBOOK

A recent survey suggested one in twenty people believe they have been abducted by aliens. One UFOlogist claims we have all been abducted at one time or another! Many victims only realize they have been abducted after their memories are drawn out by *regression therapy*. During this kind of treatment a hypnotist takes the person back to re-live events in their past. A phenomenon that involves so many people is certainly worth investigation.

ALL OF THE FOLLOWING SYMPTOMS HAVE BEEN CONSIDERED EVIDENCE OF AN ABDUCTION

- "Lost" time, in which a person can't remember what happened.
- Scars, bruises, or burns with no memory of what caused them.
- Nightmares, especially about aliens, flying, or being eaten by animals with large eyes (such as owls).
- Insomnia (not sleeping), especially when caused by fear of going to sleep.
- Medical problems, such as vomiting, headaches, tiredness, or rashes.
- Depression
- A UFO sighting
- Déjà vu (a feeling of having seen or done something before)
- A feeling of having second sight (the ability to foresee the future or see events happening elsewhere).
- An image that comes to mind over and over again (perhaps put in the brain to block memory).
- Black marks on an X-ray that don't have a known cause.

IMPLANTS

Some UFOlogists believe aliens put tracking devices in the people they abduct so that they can find them later. This device was found in the roof of an abductee's mouth. Above, 17-year-old abductee James Basel claims this was his alien tracking device.

mm

CASE STUDY 1: ANTONIO VILLAS BOAS, BRAZIL

Name/Occupation: Antonio Villas Boas. Farmer.

Date: Approx. October 16, 1957.

Location: Francisco de Sales, Brazil.

Case Description: The day after seeing a UFO, Villas Boas was alone on his tractor, plowing a field. He was dragged on board an egg-shaped craft by three aliens shaped liked humans. He was stripped, covered in a clear liquid, and had a blood sample taken from his chin.

Investigator's Notes: Villas Boas tried to fight off his abductors. Doctors found marks and scars all over his body. He suffered sickness and sleepiness that seemed like radiation poisoning. Villas Boas remembered his experience without hypnosis and never changed his story. Villas Boas remembered seeing some writing over the door of the UFO craft.

An artist's impression of Antonio's abductor and the alien craft that landed in his field.

CASE STUDY 2: BETTY AND BARNEY HILL, USA

Name/Occupation: Barney and Betty Hill. Retired social worker (Betty).

Date: September 19, 1961.

Location: Groveton, New Hampshire.

Case Description: On their way home one evening, the Hills were scared by a UFO. They later found marks on their bodies and realized they had "lost" two hours. Nightmares and depression followed. Under hypnosis they remembered being abducted by creatures with "wrap-around" eyes. Medical experiments were conducted on both Barney and Betty. Betty remembered a "star map" the aliens had shown her and drew a copy of it. From this, UFOlogists deduced the aliens came from Zeta Reticuli, about 30 light years from Earth.

Investigator's Notes: Although the Hills are often described as an "ordinary couple," Betty has had many psychic experiences. At one time, she claimed UFOs followed her everywhere. Her psychiatrist believed she was suffering delusions after a frightening experience. The doctor also thought that her husband had taken her fears into his own memory. Their abduction happened shortly after a sci-fi program on TV had shown aliens with "wrap-around" eyes.

An artist's impression of Betty and Barney during their encounter with a UFO.

CASE STUDY 3: TRAVIS WALTON, USA

Name/Occupation: Travis Walton. Logger.
Date: November 5, 1975.
Location: Apache-Sitgreaves National Forest, Arizona.

Case Description: One night in November 1975, the seven men of a logging team saw a UFO. When Walton went to investigate he was paralyzed by a beam of light from the craft. His friends ran away, leaving him for dead. Five days later, Walton turned up in a nearby town. Under hypnosis he told a classic abduction story. He was examined by three tall aliens with large eyes and was shown many UFOs.

Investigator's Notes: The Hills's abduction story had been shown on TV only a month before Walton's experience. The team were behind on their logging contract and wanted an excuse. Travis Walton was known as a practical joker. But, 25 years later, not one of the seven-man team has changed his story.

Travis Walton wrote a book. His experience was made into a film, Fire in the Sky, *in which some of the facts were changed. The team made a lot of money from their story.*

CASE STUDY 4: LINDA NAPOLITANO, USA

Name/Occupation: Linda Napolitano. Housewife.
Date: November 30, 1989.
Location: New York, New York.

Case Description: In 1989, Linda Napolitano was having hypnosis therapy because she believed she had been abducted a number of times. Under hypnosis, Linda remembered being taken out through the walls of her 12th-story apartment into a spaceship high above the streets of Manhattan. She was medically examined, then returned to her bed.

Investigator's Notes: In 1991, this story was treated seriously when two Manhattan police officers reported that they had seen a woman floating in the sky. They also saw her being taken into a UFO. The officers later claimed to be in the secret service. Another witness also claimed to have seen the event.

An artist's illustration of Linda Napolitano's abduction from her Manhattan apartment

FAKES

UFOlogy is a field that attracts con-men who want to make money. People who want to be famous also come to UFOlogy. Some of the best work to find fakes is done by responsible **UFOlogists**. They know that false claims only add to public and government skepticism. The pictures on these pages show how some of the people can be fooled some of the time.

ROSWELL REVISITED

This picture, taken in Roswell, New Mexico, was made by photographing a UFO-like object thrown toward the setting sun.

VENUSIAN SCOUT CRAFT

Effects (FX) technology has improved so much that some past fakes now look silly. This is a photograph of a "scout craft" taken by George Adamski (see page 13). It looks no more advanced than a metal lampshade and some light bulbs. What Venusian would be brave enough to set off across the solar system in one of these?

 FOOD FOR THOUGHT

UFO photographers can't win, can they? Blurred blobs are rejected as too vague to show anything. Clear images are called too good to be true. Nevertheless, after a century of UFO interest in the camera age, there is not one unquestioned, clear photograph of a UFO.

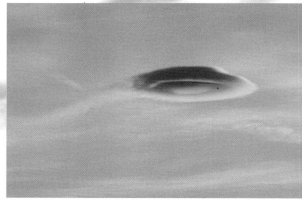

STRANGE CLOUDS, HAWAII

Photographed near Hawaii, this UFO is, in fact, a lens-shaped cloud formation. The formation is lit by the rays of the setting sun.

UFOs OVER NEW YORK

Modern FX technology makes it harder to tell the fake from the real. What is suspicious about this shot of UFOs over New York?

ALPINE FAKE, ITALY

This UFO in the Bernina Mountains is probably a table-top model that was photographed close up. The space-suited alien is almost certainly a toy soldier. It was shown to be a fake by the Italian UFO center.

AREA 51

For a long time the U.S. government claimed that Area 51 in Nevada did not exist. The area is blank on the map. In fact, it is a secret U.S. air base that may be used for testing new military aircraft. These may include unmanned aerial vehicles (*above right*). It might also be used for dumping waste from nuclear weapons. UFO-watchers regularly see craft practicing moves in the air. They believe Area 51 is where the U.S. government has stored the Roswell UFO (see pages 6–7).

A SECRET TECHNOLOGY

According to Bob Lazar, the U.S. government has recovered some crashed UFOs and is trying to figure out how their technology works.

MEN IN BLACK (MIB)

UFO witnesses have sometimes been followed by "men in black" who look like agents of the Federal Bureau of Investigation (FBI). Some UFO-believers claim the MIB are aliens trying to hide the truth. Or perhaps they are FBI agents. This MIB is from the Hollywood film of the same name.

AREA 51: CONSPIRACY

"**D**on't be fooled!" say UFO believers. "Aliens do exist. The government knows about them and has worked with them for many years. But there is a cover-up to stop you from learning the truth." To be a UFO-believer, it is almost necessary to be a conspiracy-believer. *Conspiracy* (secret plan) theories can rarely be proven or disproven. No matter what a government does or says, the conspiracy-believer shouts, "Trick!" Even when a claim is proved to be silly or a fake, conspiracy-believers simply say that they have been given bad information. They claim that the government is trying to make them look bad to make sure that others don't believe them.

BOB LAZAR

According to Bob Lazar, who claims he once worked at Area 51, the U.S. government has nine UFOs stored there. There are some problems with Lazar's story. There is no evidence that Lazar ever worked at Area 51. Also, he claims that he earned an engineering degree from a university that has no record of him. Nevertheless, his statements are often taken as proof that there is a conspiracy to cover up the truth!

MAJESTIC 12

In 1984, a TV company was sent some documents on photographic film. They seemed to prove that a group of experts called the Majestic 12 had been set up in 1947 to study the Roswell UFO. The fact that the documents had been typed on a typewriter not invented until 1963 was ignored. Conspiracy-believers still think the U.S. government has a UFO. They say if the documents were faked, they were faked by the government in an effort to mislead them!

TOP SECRET
EYES ONLY
THE WHITE HOUSE
WASHINGTON

September 24, 1947.

MEMORANDUM FOR THE SECRETARY OF DEFENSE

Dear Secretary Forrestal,

As per our recent conversation on this matter, you are hereby authorized to proceed with all due speed and caution upon your undertaking. Hereafter this matter shall be referred to only as Operation Majestic Twelve.

It continues to be my feeling that any future considerations relative to the ultimate disposition of this matter should rest solely with the Office of the President following appropriate discussions with yourself, Dr. Bush and the Director of Central Intelligence.

Harry Truman

TOP SECRET
EYES ONLY

 FOOD FOR THOUGHT

The American psychologist Elaine Showalter believes conspiracy theories are deeply damaging to society. She worries that they poison our faith in our government. We used to believe we could always ask a police officer for help. Now we feel that no matter who we elect, no government official or department can be trusted. Conspiracy-believers have made the world a frightening and lonely place.

IS ANYBODY OUT THERE?

The universe is *infinite*—it has no end. Even if life on Earth was created by chance, the universe is so big that an Earth-like planet may exist in a distant galaxy. Science fiction buffs and many UFOlogists argue that infinite space must have other life forms. Out there, they say (as any *Star Trek* fan knows), there are hundreds of different races of every possible shape, size, and color. Or are there?

MARS FACE

The *Viking* expedition to Mars in 1976 photographed a rock formation. The formation was 2 miles (3 km) long and looked like a face. Nearby there was a collection of pyramid-shaped rocks. UFOlogists claimed it was an ancient Egyptian-like civilization on the shores of a Martian sea. In 1998 the *Mars Global Surveyor* re-photographed the area from a different angle. The "Mars Face" looked like a meteor-battered mountain—exactly what it had always been.

BEYOND OUR DREAMS

Since the nearest star to Earth is 24,000,000,000,000 (24 trillion) miles away, SETI thinks it is "unlikely" aliens have visited our planet. It prefers to see UFOs as *paranormal* (cannot be explained by science) phenomena. Even so, UFOlogists still find it hard to believe that, in all the universe, there is not life out there somewhere.

LIFE ON MARS

In Antarctica in 1984, a meteorite was discovered that matched the Martian rock studied by the 1976 *Mars Viking* expedition. Scientists found tiny parts of living things and small possible fossils. The excitement is not that life exists on Mars, but that life can develop on other planets.

SETI

The Search for Extraterrestrial Intelligence (SETI) began on April 8, 1960. SETI radio telescopes at the huge Aricebo Observatory in Puerto Rico search for radio signals from the stars. On the first day, a regular "whoop, whoop" was detected from a star named Epsilon Eridani. Since then, nothing.

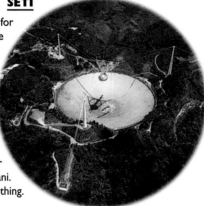

EXTRASOLAR PLANETS

This is an artist's drawing, but astronomers have discovered planets in outer space. They use the changes in a star's spectrum (the *doppler shift*) to detect "wobbles" in its spinning. These show the existence of another body in orbit around the star. In October 1997, astronomers at a Swiss observatory discovered a planet circling the star 51 Pegasi. It is half the size of Jupiter. It orbits just 4,350,000 miles (7 million km) from its star in a "year" of only four days. The surface temperature is perhaps 2,372°F (1,300°C).

In November 1961, the American radio astronomer Frank Drake gave the lecture that changed our thinking about "Is there life in space?" The answer, he said, is a mathematical equation

$$N = R^* \times f_p \times n_e \times f_l \times f_i \times f_c \times L$$

He explained that the number (N) of "space" civilizations is equal to the number of sun-type stars in the Milky Way (R*). Multiply this by the fraction of stars with planets (f_p). Then multiply that by the number of those planets that can support life (n_e). Multiply this by the fraction of planets on which life does, by chance, occur (f_l), and become intelligent (f_i), and develop an advanced scientific civilization like ours (f_c). Multiply that by the number of years that the civilization survives (L). The problem with this equation is that we don't know the value of any of the factors in it. However, we can make some reasonable guesses so that you can do the equation yourself.

1. In the Milky Way there are about 25 billion stars roughly similar to our sun (R* = 25 billion).

2. Guess that one in five has planets (so R* x f_p = 25 billion x ⅕).

3. Guess that each of those stars has two planets like Earth (n_e = 2). Further, suppose that life develops on one in a hundred (f_l = ¹⁄₁₀₀). Intelligent life develops on a tenth of those (f_i = ¹⁄₁₀). Scientific systems like ours evolve on a tenth of those (f_c = ¹⁄₁₀).

4. Guess that each of those civilizations lasts 1,000 years, in a universe that is at least 10,000 million years old, so L = a millionth (i.e., divide by a million). Work it out. How many Earthlike scientific civilizations are there in the Milky Way?

WHAT SHOULD I DO IF I MEET AN ALIEN?

Many UFO enthusiasts believe that aliens are among us. One crank on the Internet claims to have located 136 alien bases on Earth. This person claims that the bases have 14,619 aliens and a "robot army" of about 5,000 humans implanted with mind-controlling chips. Science fiction has imagined ever more frightening aliens. The *Alien* films show beings that cannot be hurt by human technology. They have acid for blood and no feelings or sense of right and wrong. They use humans as places to grow new creatures. The idea of humankind ever being visited by such beings is terrifying. So, what kind of alien are you likely to meet on the prairie on a dark and stormy night?

NORDICS

This actor from the TV series *Alien Nation* is an example of another type of alien. These are tall, Scandinavian-looking aliens from Sirius, Pleiades, or Venus. They are spiritual, gentle, and love humans. They claim their ancestors were the first human beings. But watch out! Some of them have been captured by the Greys and fitted with devices that make them slaves.

 ## FOOD FOR THOUGHT

If you meet an alien, RUN! Modern UFO writers don't claim all aliens are dangerous. Still, there is enough evidence to convince you not to take the risk. SETI has sent radio messages into space. The 1977 Voyager space probe carried the message "Greetings. We step out into the universe seeking only peaceful contact." They may as well have said, "Please come and eat us!" A common feature of abduction reports is that the aliens take small, meaningless things from humans. In one story, aliens stole a bunch of flowers from a woman. In another, they took fishing flies and money. So, if you can't run from the aliens, be sure to have something on you. It might hold their attention while you get away!

CHUPACABRAS (goat-eaters)

This group of aliens are said to live in the caves of Puerto Rico. Measuring a little over 3 feet (1 meter) tall, they have huge red eyes, fangs, long claws, and vampire-wings. They come out at night to mutilate, kill, and eat livestock. Some UFOlogists think they are the crew of a crashed spaceship. They could also be creatures that escaped into the jungle when a hurricane destroyed a secret government research center.

MIDGET MARTIANS

Like these midgets from the film *The Man in the Moon*, aliens may be from a highly developed civilization. They might be loving and lovable. They might even create a world of health and happiness!

THE GREYS

Greys are the aliens typical of most abduction stories. They are about 4½ feet (1½ meters) tall with large heads and wrap-around eyes. They come from Andromeda or Zeta Reticuli. Their military society wants to conquer Earth and make us their slaves. They have no feelings, and do their medical and genetic experiments without pain killers.

THE WORLD'S MYSTERIES EXPLORED

FATE

JANUARY 1978 75¢

DEATH BY
HELL'S FIRE

CLOSE ENCOUNTERS OF THE THIRD KIND

REPORT A UFO
AT YOUR OWN RISK

...Plus Many Other
Intriguing Features

GREEN-SKINNED MONSTERS

Reports say that UFOs can "turn off" human technology and shoot down military planes. They have paralyzing beams and can abduct whole armies of men. They do nasty experiments on people. If they exist, these beings are far more advanced than we are. And they are dangerous!

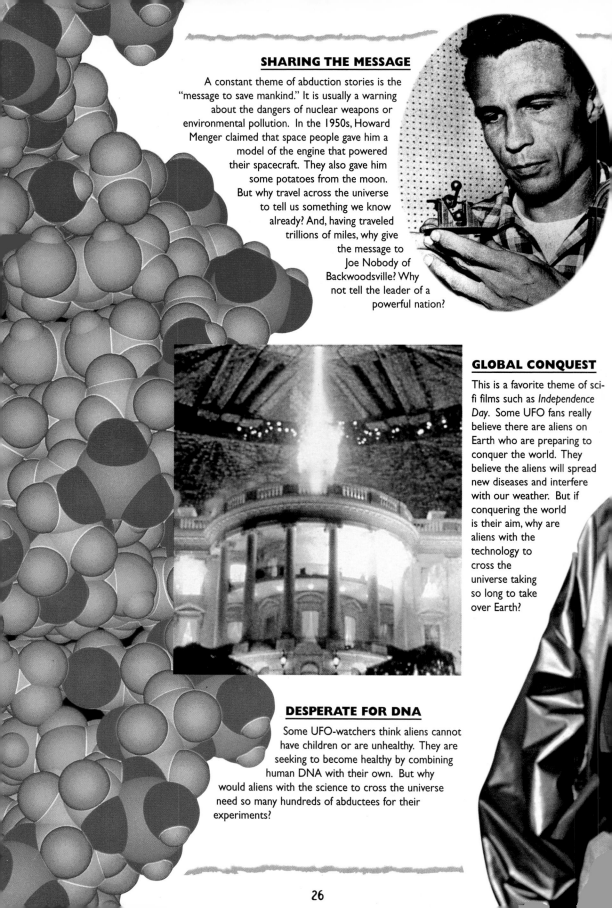

SHARING THE MESSAGE

A constant theme of abduction stories is the "message to save mankind." It is usually a warning about the dangers of nuclear weapons or environmental pollution. In the 1950s, Howard Menger claimed that space people gave him a model of the engine that powered their spacecraft. They also gave him some potatoes from the moon. But why travel across the universe to tell us something we know already? And, having traveled trillions of miles, why give the message to Joe Nobody of Backwoodsville? Why not tell the leader of a powerful nation?

GLOBAL CONQUEST

This is a favorite theme of sci-fi films such as *Independence Day*. Some UFO fans really believe there are aliens on Earth who are preparing to conquer the world. They believe the aliens will spread new diseases and interfere with our weather. But if conquering the world is their aim, why are aliens with the technology to cross the universe taking so long to take over Earth?

DESPERATE FOR DNA

Some UFO-watchers think aliens cannot have children or are unhealthy. They are seeking to become healthy by combining human DNA with their own. But why would aliens with the science to cross the universe need so many hundreds of abductees for their experiments?

WHY ARE THEY HERE?

The main flaw in all stories of alien visitors is how they got here. One respected UFOlogist thinks there are alien civilizations in the galaxy, but that the nearest one is 2,000 light years away. Traveling at the speed of light sounds possible in science fiction. In reality, the technology to "fold space" seems impossible. The speed of light is so fast that in the time it took for you to think "I want to stop" you would have passed your target. And, given the difficulty of getting here, why should aliens want to visit Earth? What have we got that they could possibly want? Until we meet one who can tell us, there are a lot of theories! Some of them are shown on these pages.

SCIENTIFIC EXPERIMENTS

Some UFO fans believe the human race is a huge genetic experiment. Some think that aliens have no feelings. For this reason, they want to study human feelings such as love, fear, and pain. This cover picture from a 1935 magazine shows that these ideas have a long history.

INTER-GALACTIC TOURISM

In the film *Morons from Outer Space* a group of extra-terrestrial tourists bump into Earth. The movie suggests another possible reason aliens visit Earth. Perhaps Earth is a galactic wildlife sanctuary run by aliens. Their rangers come to check that the human animals are healthy. Visitors are meant to stay out of sight. However, sometimes they become curious and people see them.

FOOD FOR THOUGHT

The problem with all of these theories is that it would take very advanced technology to cross the universe to get to Earth. But the aliens don't seem to make any progress once they arrive. They might come as scientific human-watchers trying to stay hidden. Or maybe they are conquerors trying to defeat us. Another possibility is that they are do-gooders with a message to share. After 50 years, the aliens have proved unable to reach any of these goals!

TIME-SLIP

Occasionally, radio waves seem to "wobble" and listeners find their program interrupted briefly by a different station. We think of time as a knife-edge with an empty space before it and nothing behind it. But if time were like a radio signal that can sometimes wobble, UFOs might be a random peek into the future. Time-slip would also explain things like sightings of the Loch Ness monster, ghosts, and the "walking dead." It would also supply a reason for such strange experiences as *déjà vu*, in which we have a feeling of something having happened before.

THEORIES

Some **UFOlogists** think the popular definition of an alien as an extraterrestrial (ET) is wrong. Today, most **UFOlogists** accept it is unlikely that Earth is being visited from other galaxies. Instead, they prefer to define alien as "something outside normal human experience." Perhaps, some say, aliens are spiritual expressions. In the 1950s, Richard Miller, claimed an alien from Alpha Centauri told him UFOs were angels. Other people believe UFOs are demons. The founder of the Aetherius Society, George King, claimed Jesus Christ was an alien from Venus. King was a London taxi driver who claimed he was recruited by aliens in 1954 to help save the world. Other UFOlogists argue that UFO experiences are a real phenomenon. However, they seek explanations that do not involve little green men in spaceships!

THE "OZ" FACTOR

Known as the Oz factor, a still and eerie quiet is often reported to happen just before an alien meeting. UFOlogist Jenny Randles points out the ways UFO events are like paranormal phenomena. These phenomena include extra-sensory perception (ESP), out-of-body experiences, and near-death experiences. She thinks that there might be other beings in the universe. Randles believes these aliens might be trying to get in touch on a psychic level.

ANOTHER DIMENSION

UFO experiences may be related to our three-dimensional world. Earth has three dimensions: length, width, and height. A creature living in a two-dimensional world would have no height, only length and width (like a sheet of paper). Such a creature would not be able to see up or down. "Up" and "down" would not exist in its two-dimensional world. Maybe alien worlds have more than three dimensions. If Earth shares space with and occasionally overlaps these kinds of other-dimensional worlds, then glimpses of these would be very puzzling for us.

WAKING DREAMS

These experiences can be so clear that they seem real. Even after they wake up, the dreamer may have trouble telling the difference between their dream and reality. Many waking dreams are confusing, terrifying events. Later, the brain tries to come to terms with the shock. It might try to explain the dream. In the past, people blamed ghosts or demons for their visions. Today, because sci-fi images and advanced technology are familiar to us, our brain is likely to use aliens to explain such experiences.

 FOOD FOR THOUGHT

These ideas are a retreat from UFOlogy as scientific fact, into UFO-faith. In UFO faith, you can't prove anything, but simply believe it. No one has been able to prove that extraterrestrial spacecraft exist.

WHY ARE WE SO INTERESTED?

In 1960, two French writers, Jacques Bergier and Louis Pauwels, published *The Morning of the Magicians*. This book argued that science didn't have all the answers. The authors said that society was like a car speeding along a highway. It was going somewhere all right, but what about the fields and villages on either side? They suggested that because of technology, humankind was missing many of the important truths about life. The book revived interest in experiences that couldn't be scientifically explained. Maybe part of the reason people are so interested in UFOs is that they are a mystery. The many theories about them do not yet explain them away.

ESCAPISM

Prince Gautama Siddhartha (Buddha) lived in a palace and never saw the real world. One day, he went out and was so horrified by the suffering he saw that he left the palace forever. Today, we see the sadness of the world on television all the time. In a sense, we enjoy "going back into the palace." We like getting away from reality and into a fantasy world.

 FOOD FOR THOUGHT

Interest in UFOs and stories about alien encounters is probably here to stay. We are naturally fascinated by the unknown and the frightening. Extraterrestrial UFOs can never be disproved. This is because science can only prove that something does exist, not that it doesn't.

THE MARTIANS ARE COMING!

In 1938, a radio adaptation of *The War of the Worlds*, a book by H. G. Wells, was so realistic it created panic when broadcast in America. Despite regular announcements that it was only a play, some people believed aliens were invading. William Dock, 76, from Grover's Mill, New Jersey, (where Martians had supposedly landed) was ready with a shotgun to scare off the invaders. People seemed almost to want the story to be true!

CLASS
Illus
Featuring St
World's Grea
No. 124 15¢

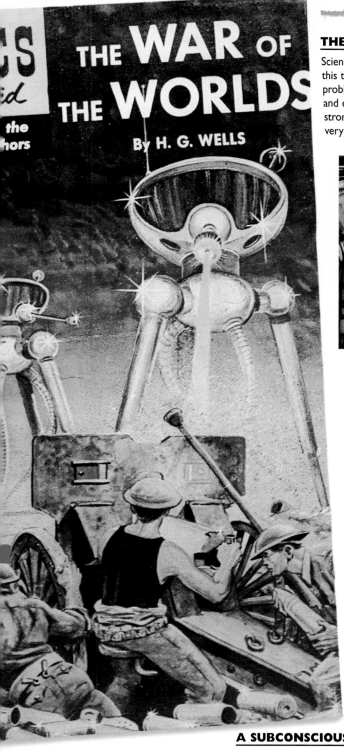

THE WAR OF THE WORLDS
By H. G. WELLS

THE RISE OF SCI-FI

Science fiction began in the nineteenth century. At this time it seemed that science would solve all problems. Readers found it interesting, frightening, and exciting. Today, interest in science fiction is stronger than ever. Programs like *Star Trek* are very popular.

THE SEARCH FOR SOMETHING BEYOND OURSELVES

The psychological (mental) need for "something out there" that is bigger than we are is as old as humankind. The need to believe in something beyond ourselves is strong. It can lead to belief in the paranormal. Interest in UFOs is perhaps part of this. One example is the Aetherius Society (see page 29). Another is the *Urantia Book*, which was written in the 1930s by Dr. William Sadler. Sadler was a psychiatrist who also studied religions. The *Urantia Book* teaches that the universe is full of many beings— gods, angels, and mortals (including human beings). It is not a religion, but people do attend study fellowships about it.

A SUBCONSCIOUS IMAGE

In his 1958 book *Flying Saucers, a Modern Myth*, the great psychologist Carl Jung called UFOs a "rumor." He said UFOs appeal to our subconscious. Even their circular shape is a powerful subconscious image. He said UFOs represent both our hope that science and technology will save us, and our fear that it will destroy us. He concluded that to be fascinated by UFOs is a natural and expected part of our psychology.

DID YOU KNOW?

After a UFO sighting, web-like strands called "angel hair" are often found at the site. A false image on a radar screen is also called an "angel" (or ghost).

Some UFOlogists believe that UFOs are see-through creatures that live in the sky. They believe that the creatures have not been discovered yet.

Many abducted people describe aliens with similar features. They say that the aliens look like half-human babies with some alien DNA.

One government study of unexplained events in the sky was called "Project Twinkle." It had only one camera and failed to photograph a single UFO.

Some people claim they can "channel" the voices of aliens through their own bodies. This claim is like that of a medium who speaks on behalf of the dead.

A "flap" is the publicity surrounding a UFO sighting. A "wave" is a number of sightings from all over the world in a short time. A "hot spot" is a place where UFOs are often seen.

Some people claim to be able to "see" events and objects far away by using paranormal powers. Sometimes, they "see" UFOs over the objects.

The government of the former Soviet Union took UFOs very seriously. They organized a series of studies. Russia even has its own "Area 51." It is in an area in the Ural Mountains known as the "M-zone."

One UFOlogist claims that UFOs move by creating an electrical and gravitational field. By changing the field strength, they can move up or down at great speeds.

You can find out lots more about UFOs on the Internet. Why not check out these Web sites?

UFO EVIDENCE http://www.ufoevidence.org/

MUFON http://www.mufon.com/

BUFORA (The British UFO Research Organization) http://www.bufora.org.uk

Robert Sheaffer's The UFO Skeptic's Page http://www.debunker.com/ufo.html

UFO Resource Center http://www.uforc.com/

SETI Institute http://www.seti-inst.edu

First published in Great Britain by ticktock Publishing Ltd. Printed in China.

ISBN-13: 978-1-59905-441-4   ISBN-10: 1-59905-441-8   eBook: 978-1-60291-767-5

15 14 13 12 11   1 2 3 4 5

Picture Credits: t = top, b = bottom, c = center, l = left, r = right, OFC = outside front cover, OBC = outside back cover, IFC = inside front cover

Alastair Carew-Cox; 31cr. Ann Ronan/Image Select; 3b, 31br. Corbis; 24b & OBC; 20bl. Corbis Royalty Free Image; 2/3cb, 4b, 4c, 5bl, 6/7b, 7tr, 8br, 8bl, 8/9b, 10tl, 11c, 10./11b, 10/11t, 12c, 12tl, 12/13b, 12/13t, 13br, 15tr, 21tl, 24/25c, 26tr, 30/31t. FPG International; 18/19t. Giraudon; 30tl. Images; 2/3t, 25r & OFC (inset pic), 29r. K Evans Picture Library; 2cl, 4/5c & 5cr, 8/9b, 10c, 16cr, 16br, 17br, 18bl, 25bl, 27tr. Norio Hayakawa, Groomwatch; 6/7t & OFC (main pic), 7cr, 18tl, 22/23, 22cb, 22/23cb, 22tl, 22ct, 26l. Telegraph Colour Library; 28/2

Every effort has been made to trace the copyright holders and we apologize in advance for any unintent
We would be pleased to insert the appropriate acknowledgement in any subsequent edition of this p

SADDLEBACK
EDUCATIONAL PUBLISHING